Donald Trump. Even his most loyal supporters know all about his track record with **women** - and the **utter disregard** with which he holds the traditional institution of **marriage.**

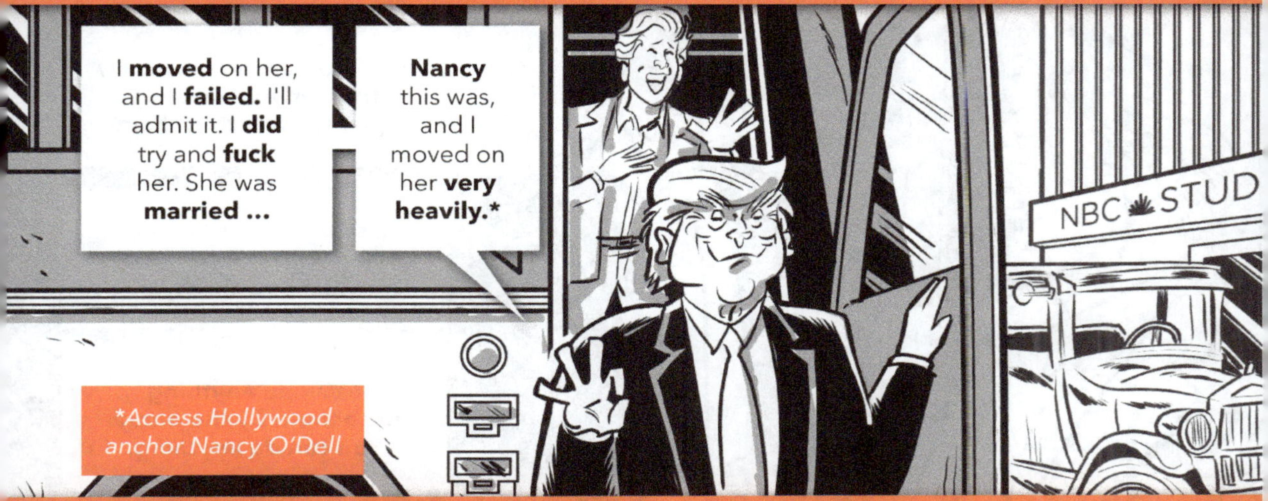
I **moved** on her, and I **failed.** I'll admit it. I **did** try and **fuck** her. She was **married ...**
Nancy this was, and I moved on her **very heavily.***
NBC STUD
*Access Hollywood anchor Nancy O'Dell

They **know** he cheats - they just don't **care.** A lot of them even **admire** him for it. But, when facing an **opponent -** one whose husband had **also** been exposed as unfaithful - the tone **changed ...**

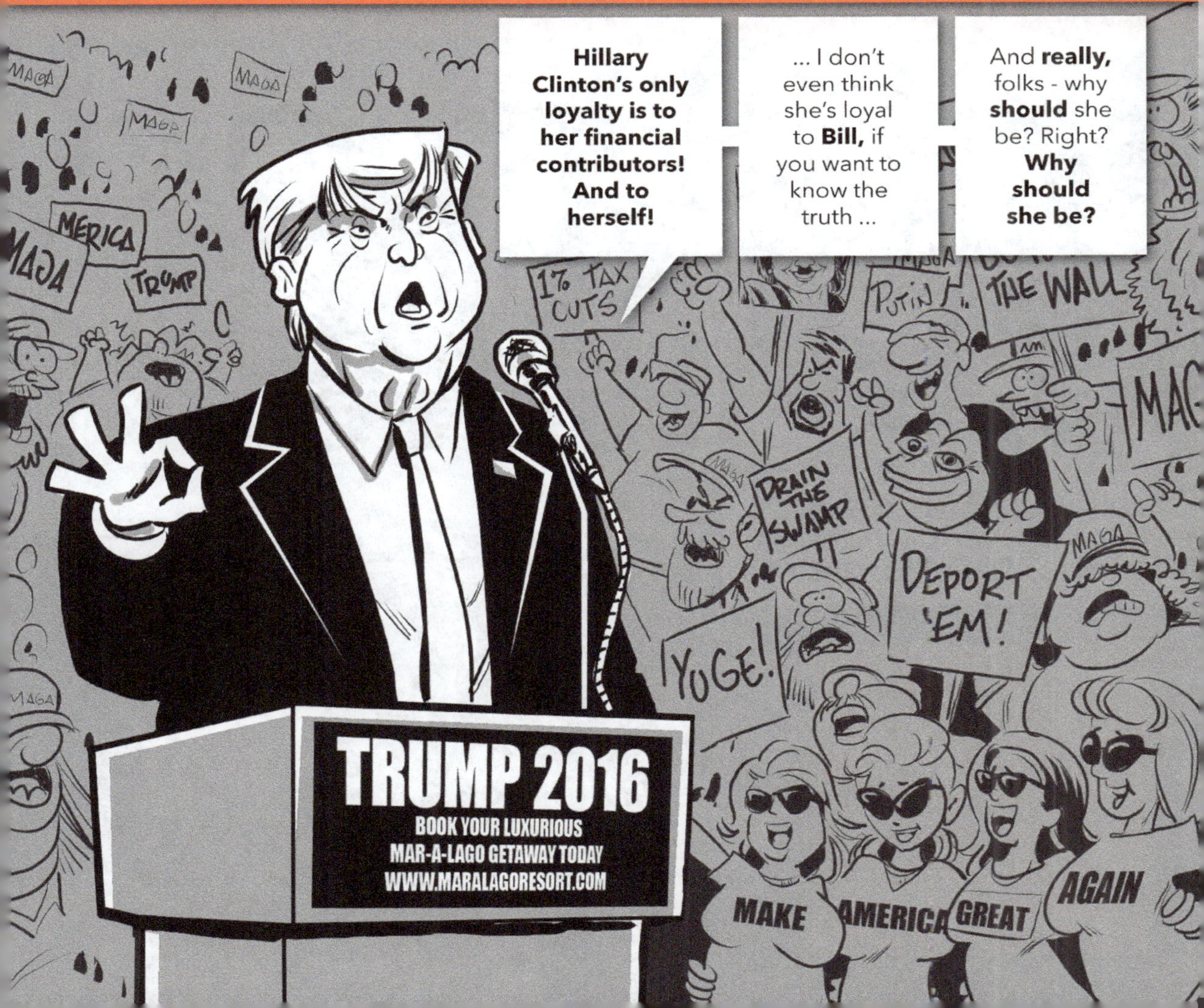
Hillary Clinton's only loyalty is to her financial contributors! And to herself!
... I don't even think she's loyal to **Bill,** if you want to know the truth ...
And **really,** folks - why **should** she be? Right? **Why should she be?**
MAGA
MERICA
TRUMP
1% TAX CUTS
PUTIN
THE WALL
DRAIN THE SWAMP
DEPORT 'EM!
YUGE!
TRUMP 2016
BOOK YOUR LUXURIOUS
MAR-A-LAGO GETAWAY TODAY
WWW.MARALAGORESORT.COM
MAKE AMERICA GREAT AGAIN

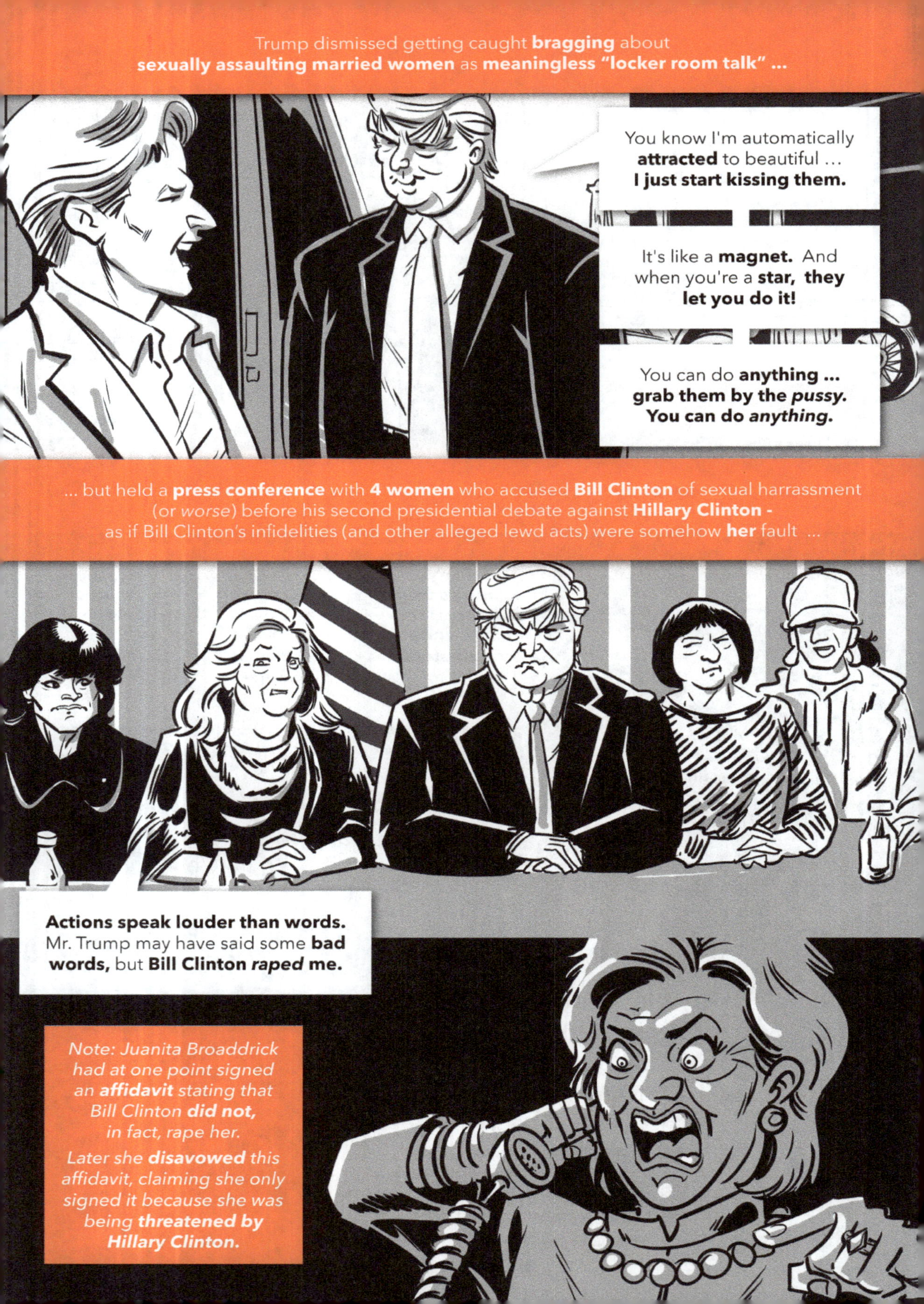
Trump dismissed getting caught **bragging** about **sexually assaulting married women** as **meaningless "locker room talk" ...**
You know I'm automatically **attracted** to beautiful ... **I just start kissing them.**
It's like a **magnet.** And when you're a **star, they let you do it!**
You can do **anything ... grab them by the *pussy.* You can do *anything.***
... but held a **press conference** with **4 women** who accused **Bill Clinton** of sexual harrassment (or *worse*) before his second presidential debate against **Hillary Clinton -** as if Bill Clinton's infidelities (and other alleged lewd acts) were somehow **her** fault ...
Actions speak louder than words. Mr. Trump may have said some **bad words,** but **Bill Clinton *raped* me.**
*Note: Juanita Broaddrick had at one point signed an **affidavit** stating that Bill Clinton **did not,** in fact, rape her.*
*Later she **disavowed** this affidavit, claiming she only signed it because she was being **threatened by Hillary Clinton.***

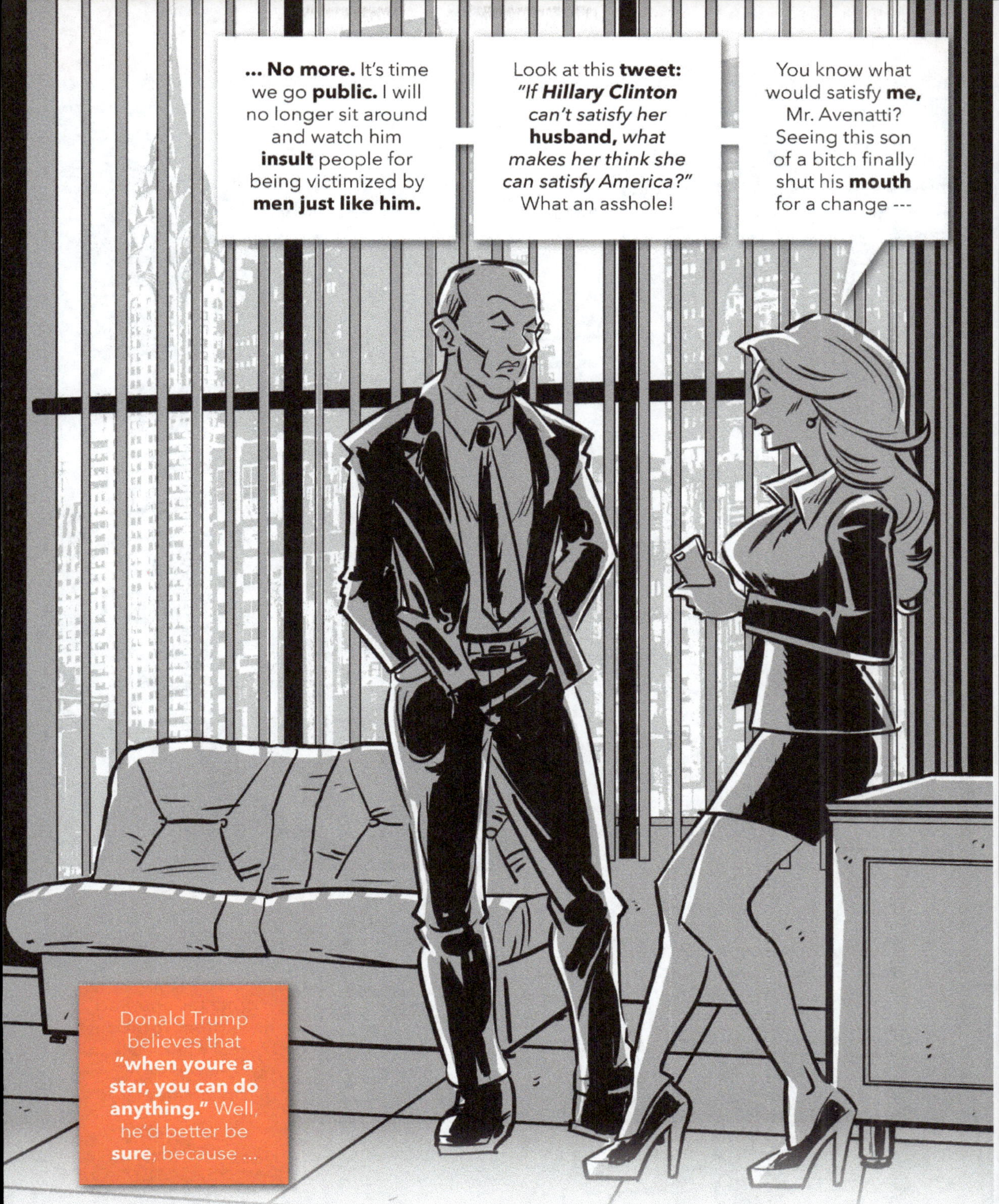
... **No more.** It's time we go **public.** I will no longer sit around and watch him **insult** people for being victimized by **men just like him.**
Look at this **tweet:** *"If* ***Hillary Clinton*** *can't satisfy her* ***husband,*** *what makes her think she can satisfy America?"* What an asshole!
You know what would satisfy **me,** Mr. Avenatti? Seeing this son of a bitch finally shut his **mouth** for a change ---
Donald Trump believes that **"when youre a star, you can do anything."** Well, he'd better be **sure**, because ...

STORMY'S COMING

WRITTEN AND ILLUSTRATED BY JOE PARADISE

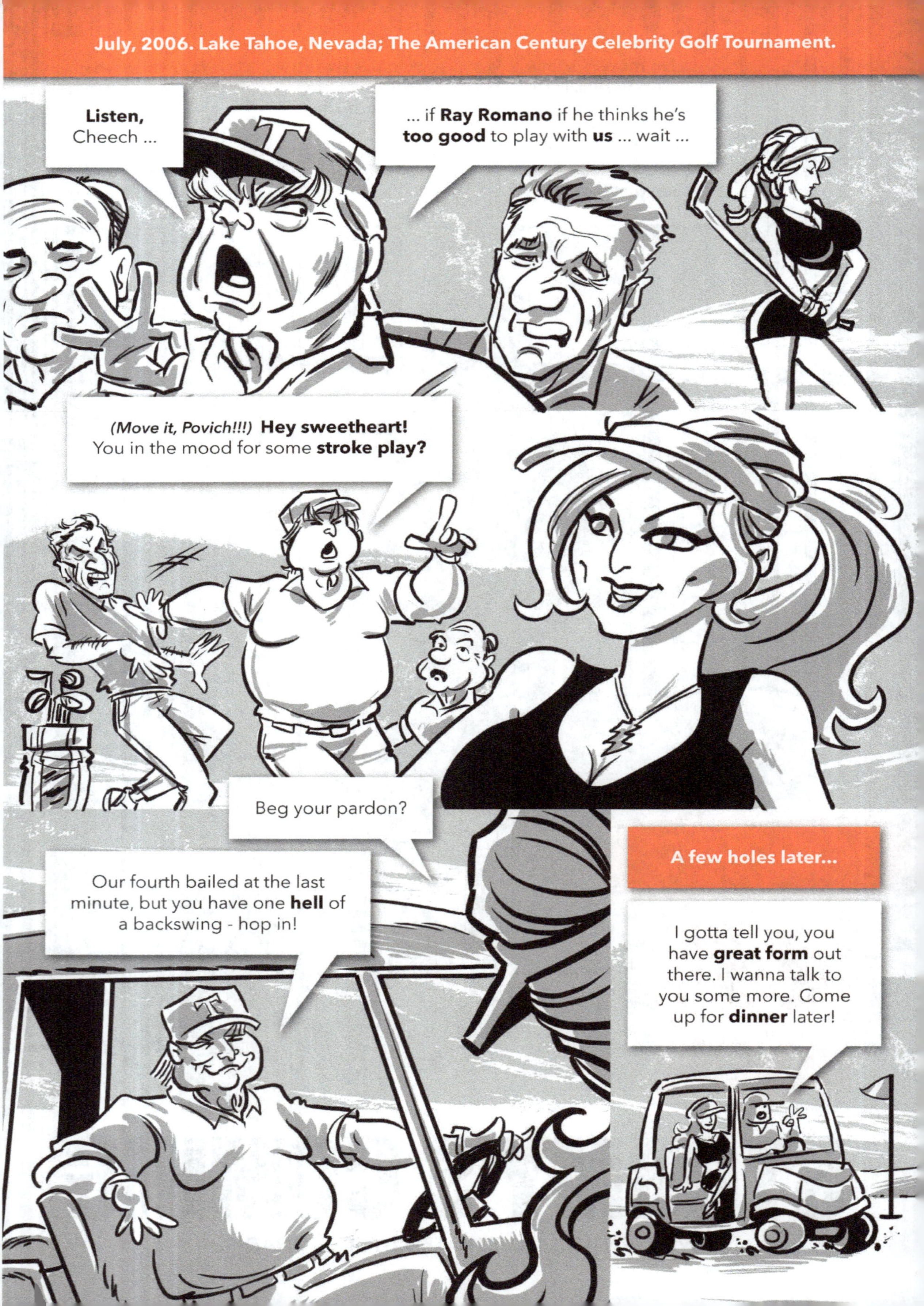
July, 2006. Lake Tahoe, Nevada; The American Century Celebrity Golf Tournament.
Listen, Cheech ...
... if Ray Romano if he thinks he's too good to play with us ... wait ...
(Move it, Povich!!!) Hey sweetheart! You in the mood for some stroke play?
Beg your pardon?
Our fourth bailed at the last minute, but you have one hell of a backswing - hop in!
A few holes later...
I gotta tell you, you have great form out there. I wanna talk to you some more. Come up for dinner later!

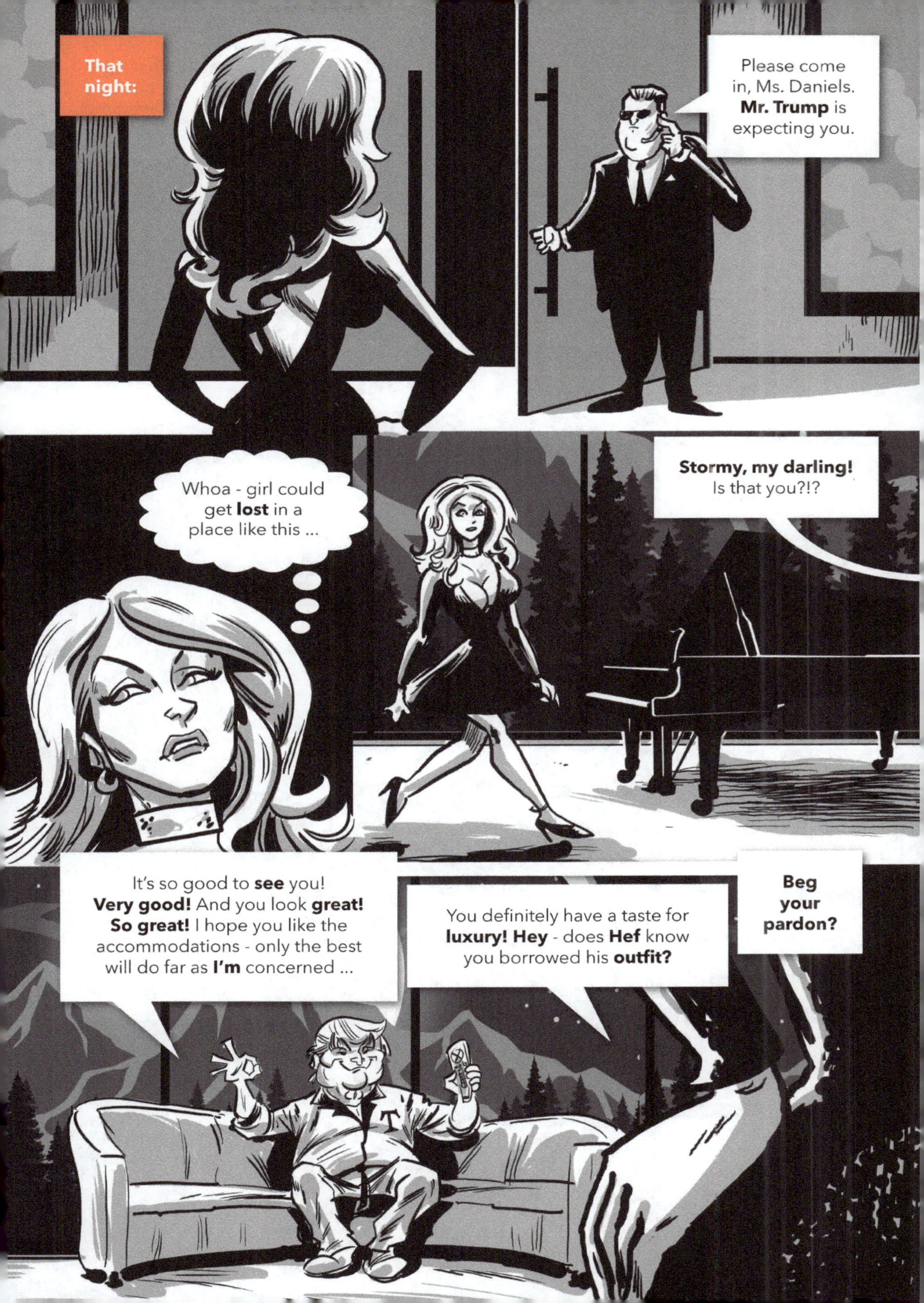
That night:
Please come in, Ms. Daniels. **Mr. Trump** is expecting you.
Whoa - girl could get **lost** in a place like this ...
Stormy, my darling! Is that you?!?
It's so good to **see** you! **Very good!** And you look **great! So great!** I hope you like the accommodations - only the best will do far as **I'm** concerned ...
You definitely have a taste for **luxury! Hey** - does **Hef** know you borrowed his **outfit?**
Beg your pardon?

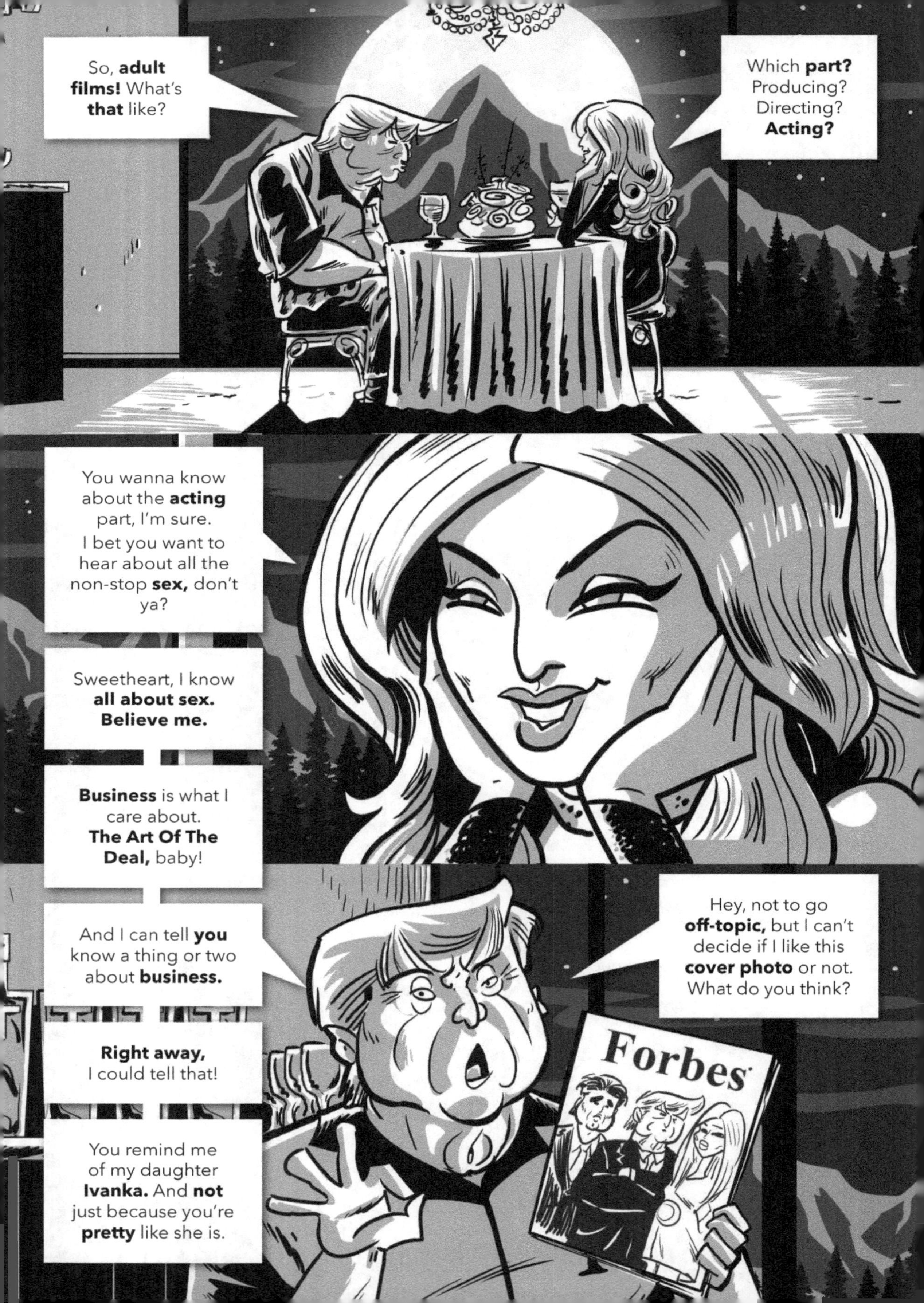

So, **adult films!** What's **that** like?
Which **part?** Producing? Directing? **Acting?**
You wanna know about the **acting** part, I'm sure. I bet you want to hear about all the non-stop **sex,** don't ya?
Sweetheart, I know **all about sex. Believe me.**
Business is what I care about. **The Art Of The Deal,** baby!
And I can tell **you** know a thing or two about **business.**
Right away, I could tell that!
You remind me of my daughter **Ivanka.** And **not** just because you're **pretty** like she is.
Hey, not to go **off-topic,** but I can't decide if I like this **cover photo** or not. What do you think?
Forbes

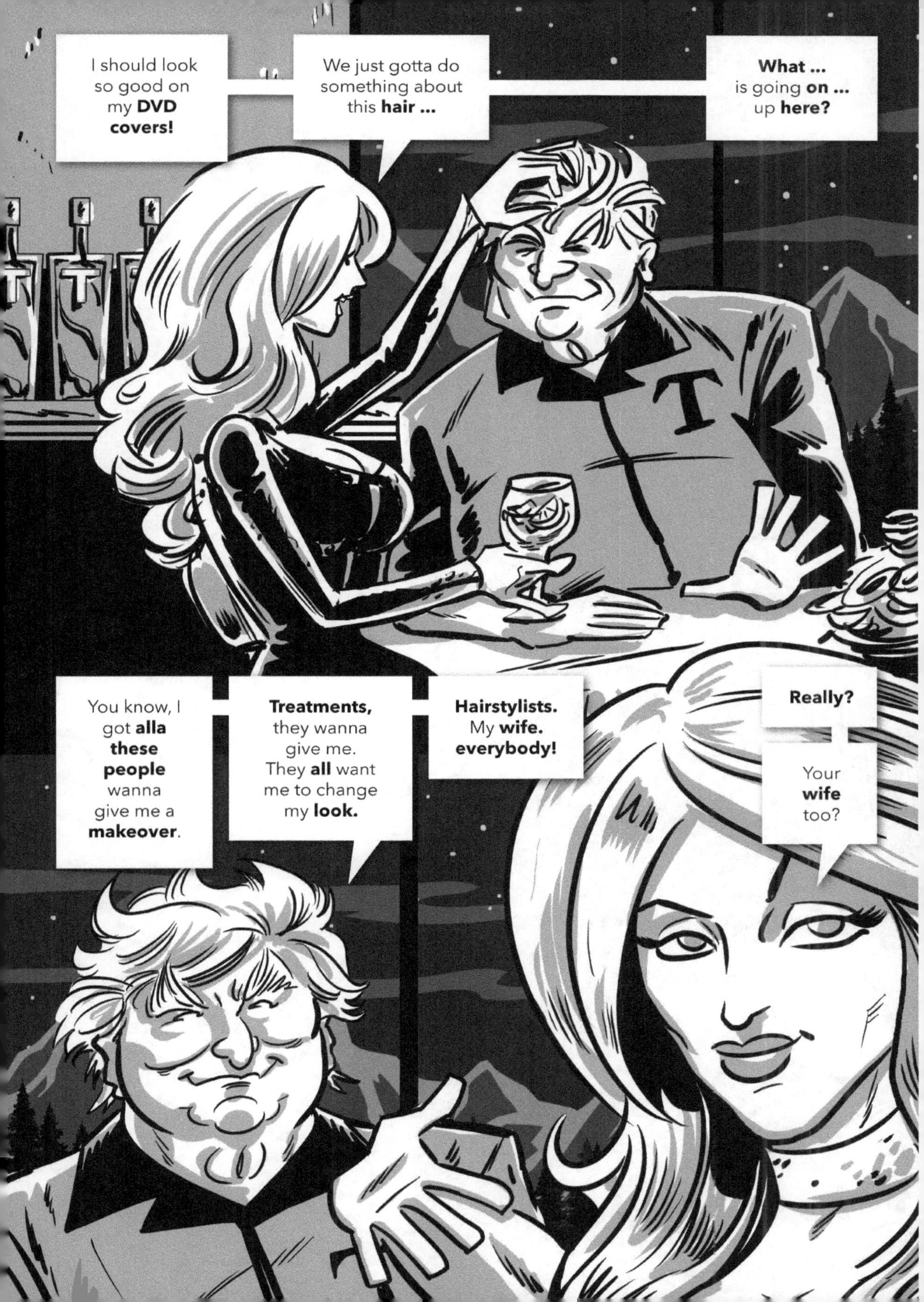
I should look so good on my **DVD covers!**
We just gotta do something about this **hair ...**
What ... is going **on ...** up **here?**
You know, I got **alla these people** wanna give me a **makeover**.
Treatments, they wanna give me. They **all** want me to change my **look.**
Hairstylists. My **wife. everybody!**
Really?
Your **wife** too?

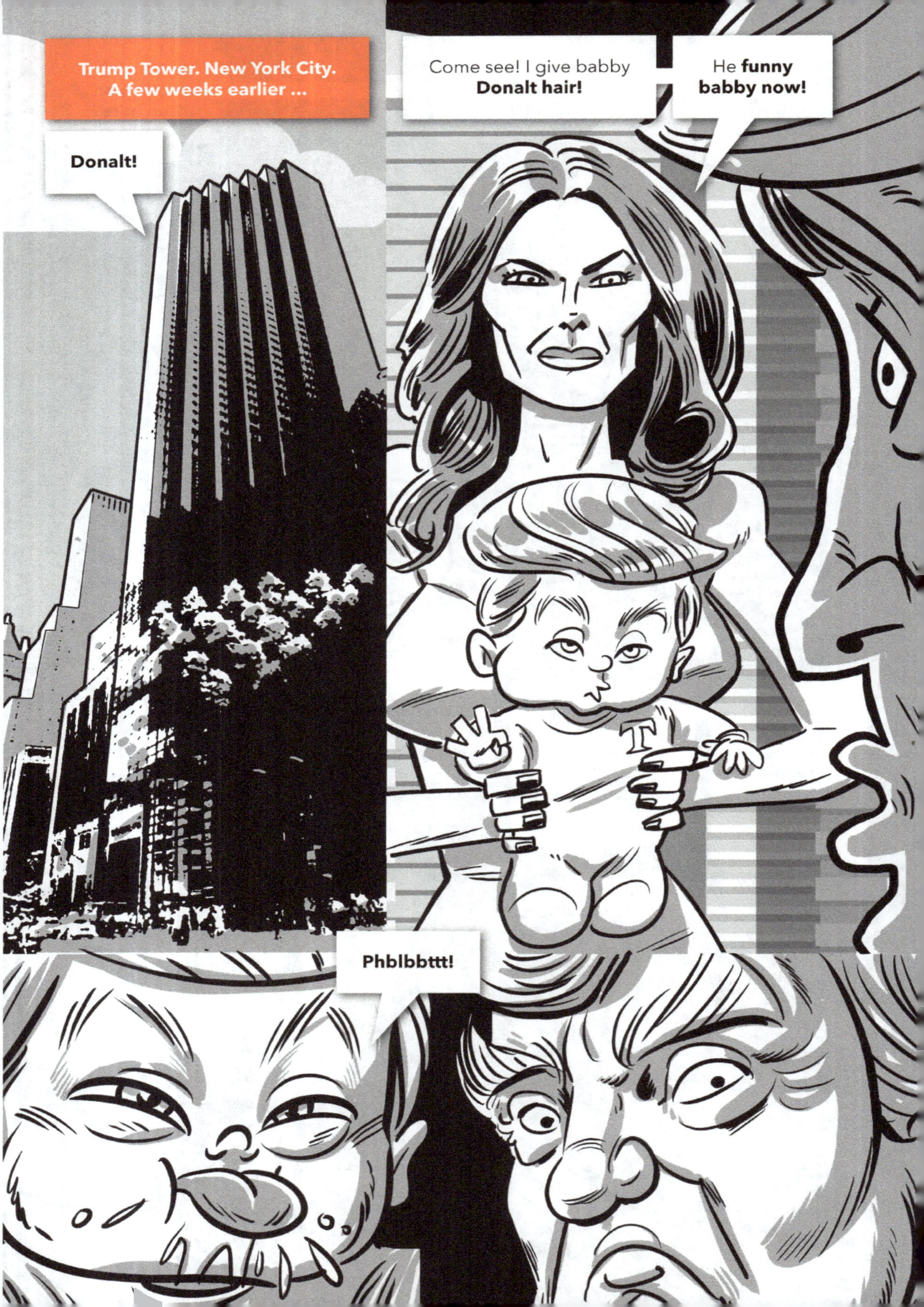

Trump Tower. New York City.
A few weeks earlier ...
Donalt!
Come see! I give babby **Donalt hair!**
He **funny babby now!**
Phblbbttt!

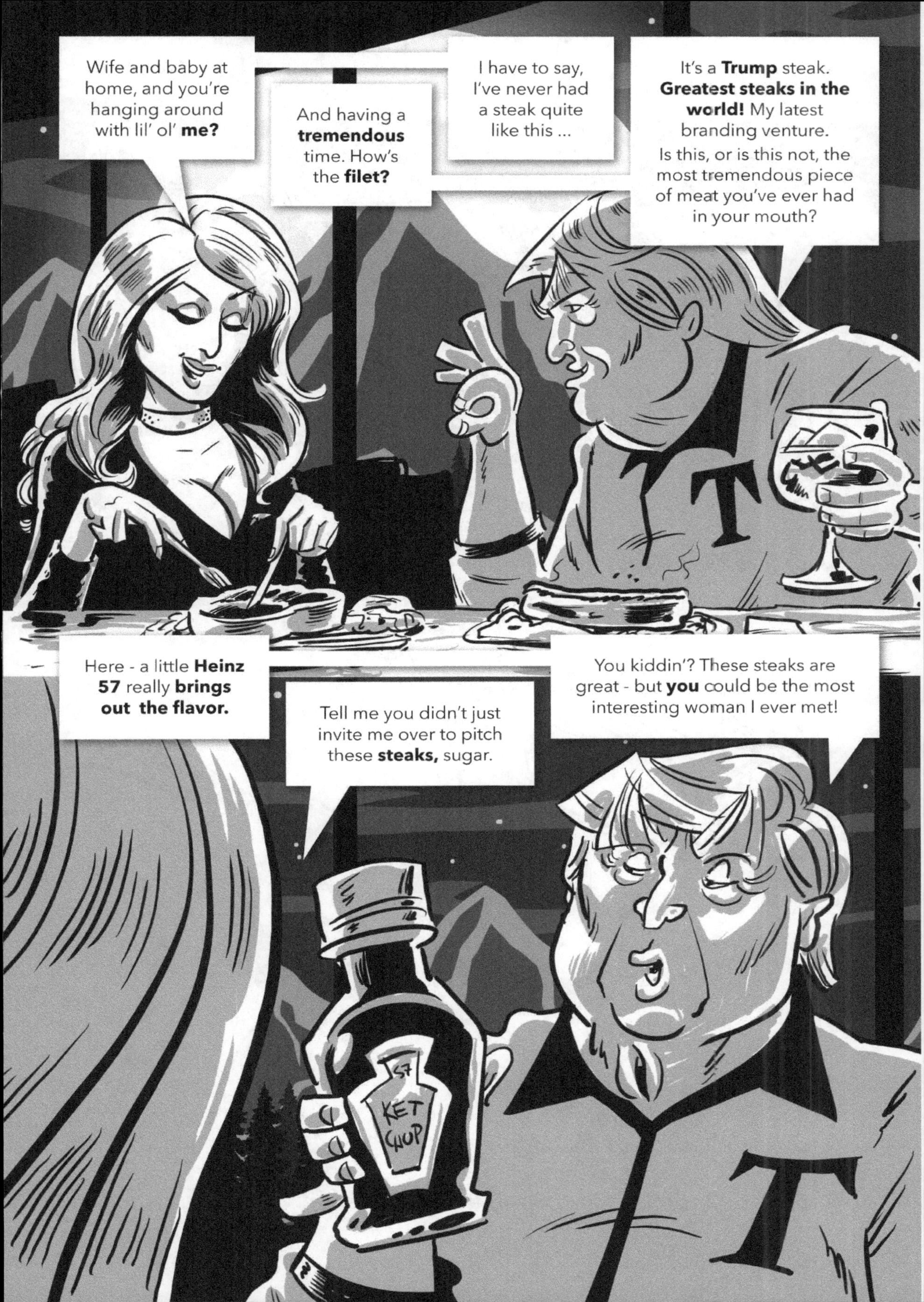
Wife and baby at home, and you're hanging around with lil' ol' **me?**
And having a **tremendous** time. How's the **filet?**
I have to say, I've never had a steak quite like this ...
It's a **Trump** steak. **Greatest steaks in the world!** My latest branding venture.
Is this, or is this not, the most tremendous piece of meat you've ever had in your mouth?
Here - a little **Heinz 57** really **brings out the flavor.**
Tell me you didn't just invite me over to pitch these **steaks,** sugar.
You kiddin'? These steaks are great - but **you** could be the most interesting woman I ever met!
57
KET CHUP

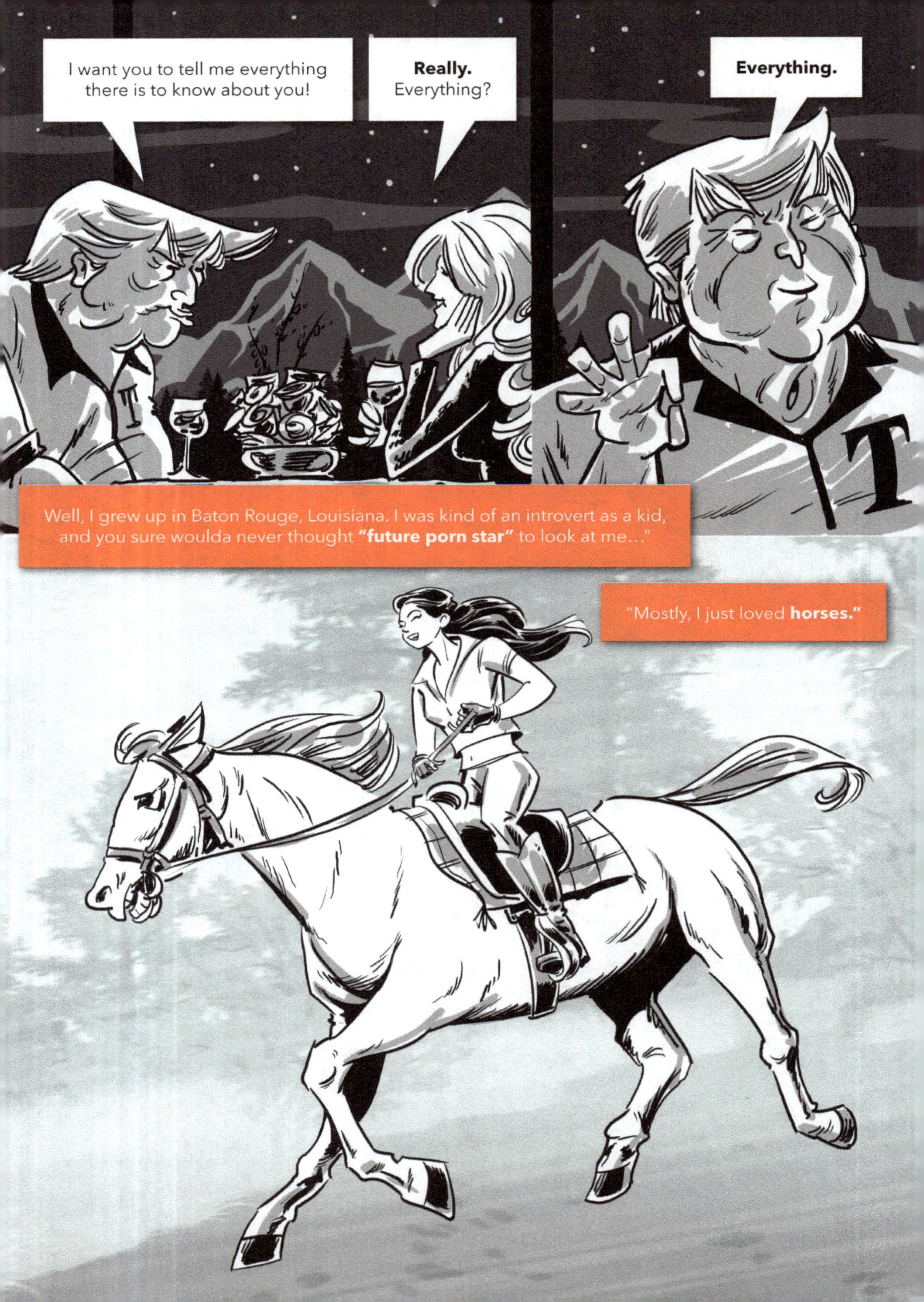
I want you to tell me everything there is to know about you!
Really. Everything?
Everything.
Well, I grew up in Baton Rouge, Louisiana. I was kind of an introvert as a kid, and you sure woulda never thought **"future porn star"** to look at me..."
"Mostly, I just loved **horses."**

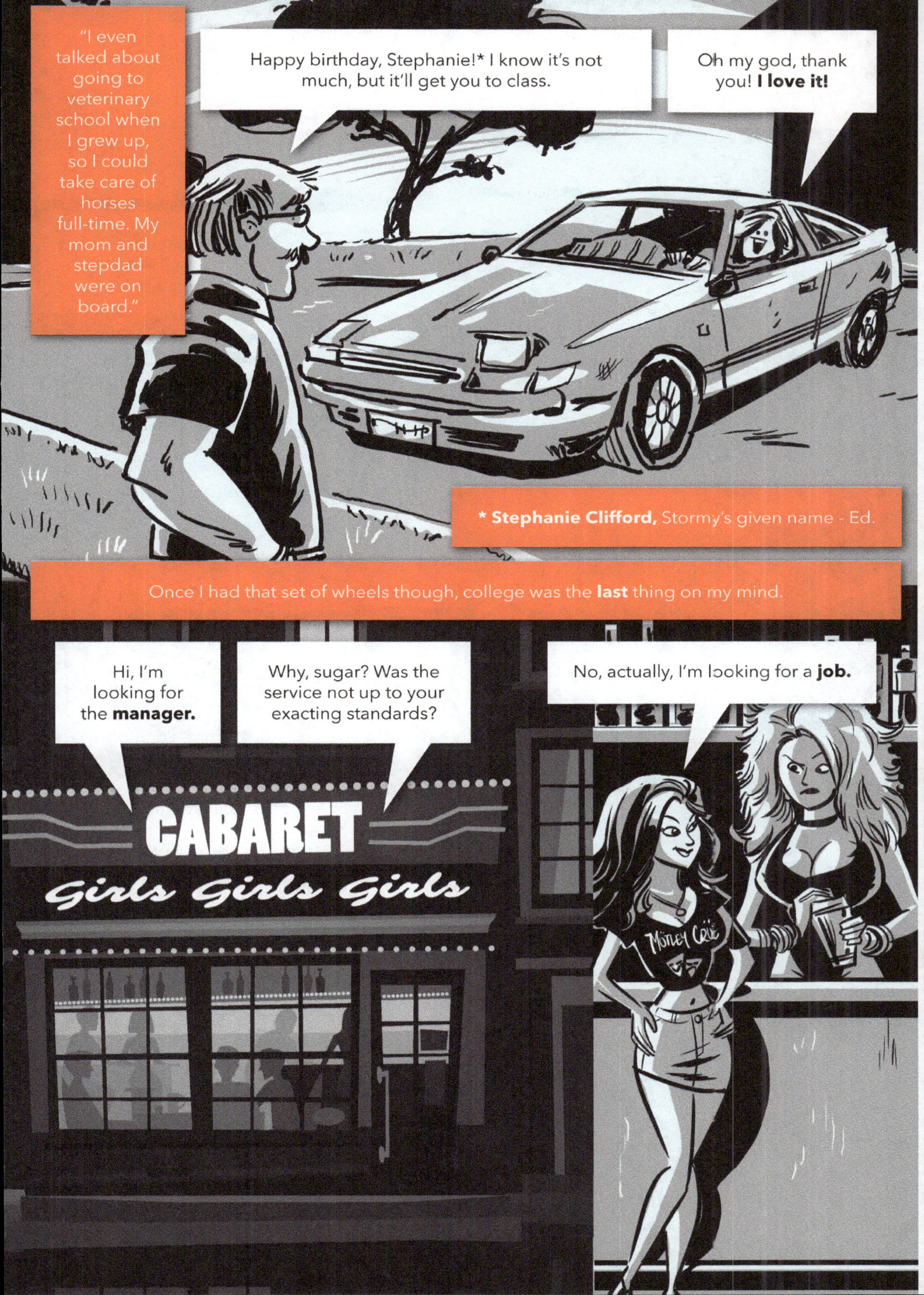
"I even talked about going to veterinary school when I grew up, so I could take care of horses full-time. My mom and stepdad were on board."
Happy birthday, Stephanie!* I know it's not much, but it'll get you to class.
Oh my god, thank you! **I love it!**
* **Stephanie Clifford,** Stormy's given name - Ed.
Once I had that set of wheels though, college was the **last** thing on my mind.
Hi, I'm looking for the **manager.**
Why, sugar? Was the service not up to your exacting standards?
No, actually, I'm looking for a **job.**
CABARET
Girls Girls Girls
MÖTLEY CRÜE

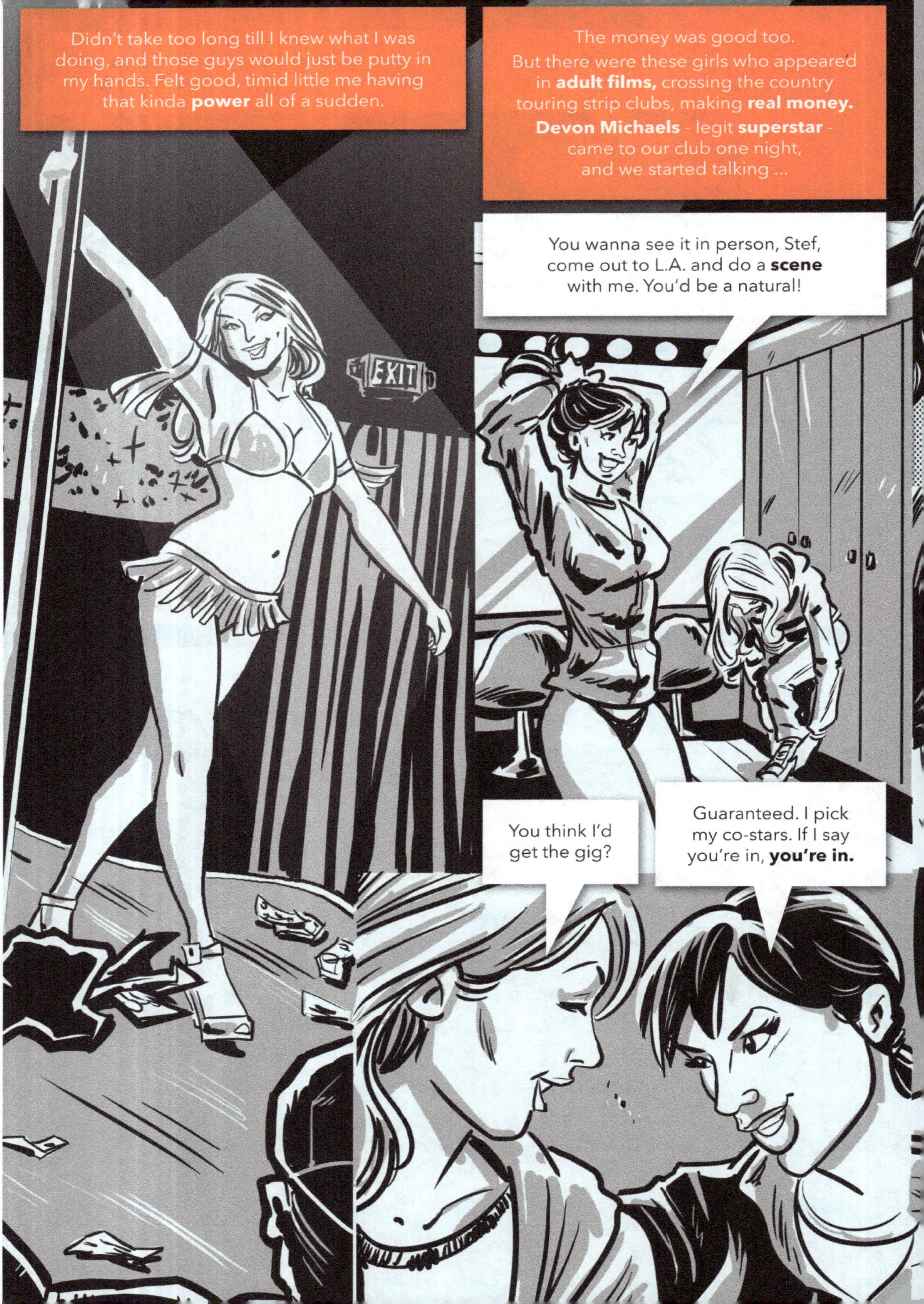
Didn't take too long till I knew what I was doing, and those guys would just be putty in my hands. Felt good, timid little me having that kinda **power** all of a sudden.
EXIT
The money was good too.
But there were these girls who appeared in **adult films,** crossing the country touring strip clubs, making **real money.**
Devon Michaels - legit **superstar** - came to our club one night, and we started talking ...
You wanna see it in person, Stef, come out to L.A. and do a **scene** with me. You'd be a natural!
You think I'd get the gig?
Guaranteed. I pick my co-stars. If I say you're in, **you're in.**

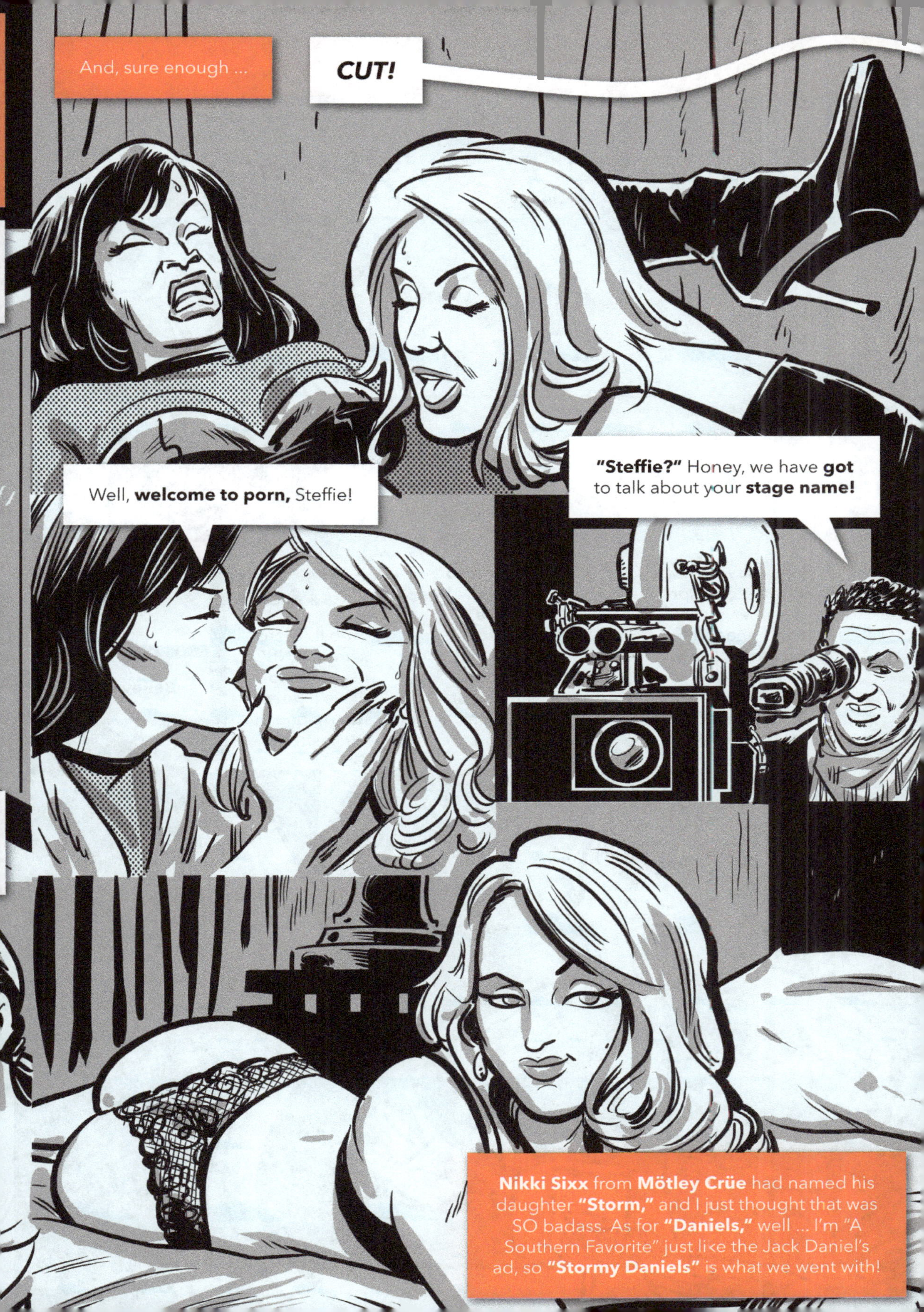
And, sure enough ...
CUT!
Well, welcome to porn, Steffie!
"Steffie?" Honey, we have got to talk about your stage name!
Nikki Sixx from Mötley Crüe had named his daughter "Storm," and I just thought that was SO badass. As for "Daniels," well ... I'm "A Southern Favorite" just like the Jack Daniel's ad, so "Stormy Daniels" is what we went with!

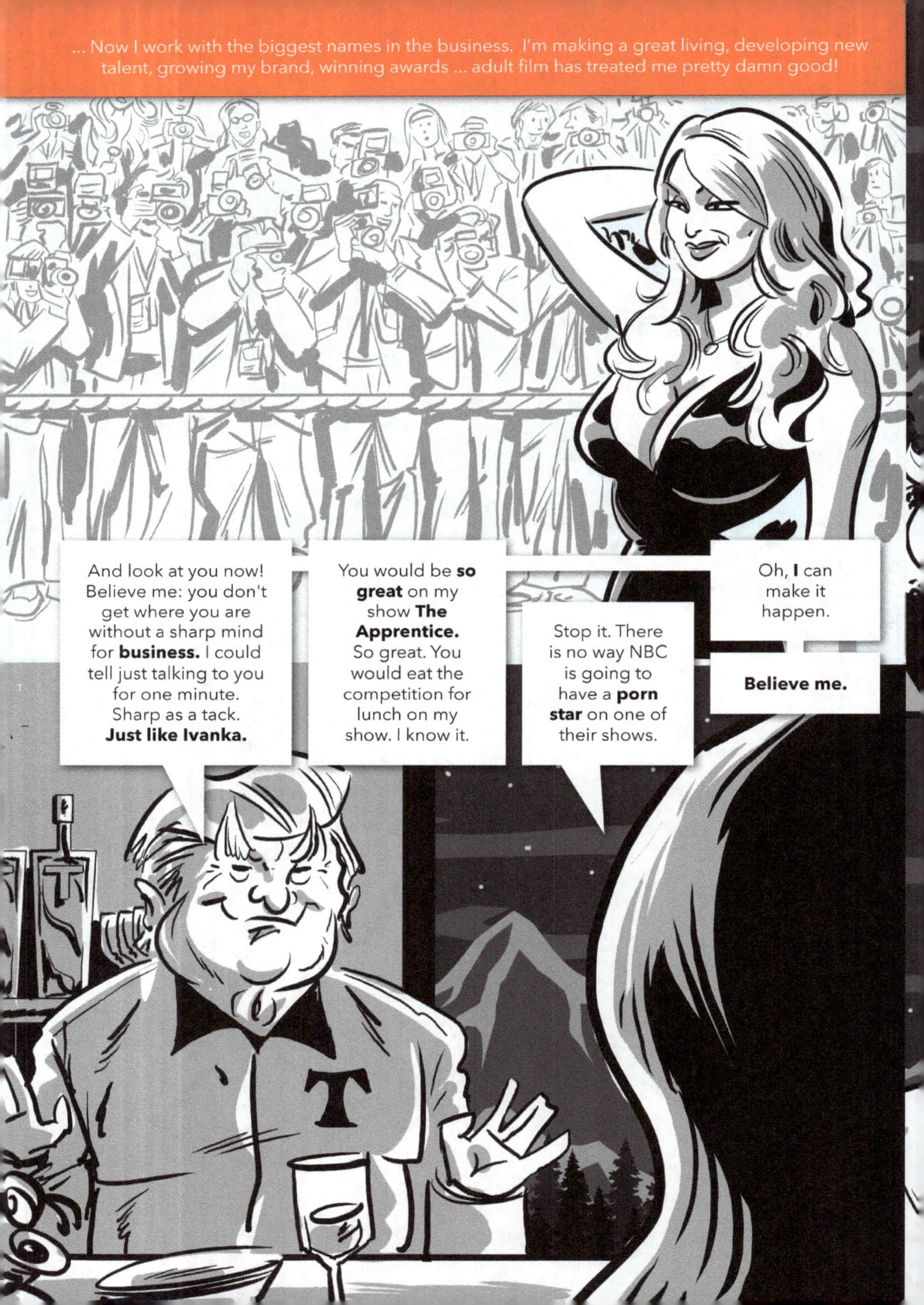
... Now I work with the biggest names in the business. I'm making a great living, developing new talent, growing my brand, winning awards ... adult film has treated me pretty damn good!
And look at you now! Believe me: you don't get where you are without a sharp mind for **business.** I could tell just talking to you for one minute. Sharp as a tack. **Just like Ivanka.**
You would be **so great** on my show **The Apprentice.** So great. You would eat the competition for lunch on my show. I know it.
Stop it. There is no way NBC is going to have a **porn star** on one of their shows.
Oh, **I** can make it happen.
Believe me.

"OK, but fair warning: if you're bullshittin' me, I'm gonna roll up this **magazine** and **spank** you with it."

"Promises, promises."

The details of what happened next are only allegations at present. According to Daniels, she **did** in fact spank him with that magazine.

She excused herself for a moment to use the rest room, and when she returned, Trump was waiting for her on the bed.

A quick and reportedly unremarkable sex session with the future President ensued.

Five years after being interviewed by InTouch magazine for a story that would not see the light of day for years after the fact, Daniels was contacted by Trump family attorney Michael Cohen. He offered her a payment of $130,000 in exchange for her silence on the Trump affair.

The contract also stipulated that she would be obligated to pay Trump $1 million for each offense should she break the agreement. She signed, but later felt morally compelled to come forward and tell her story.

Trump's lawyers came at her hard and fast with a $20 million countersuit, alleging that Ms. Daniels broke the NDA and caused Trump damages in the process.

It has to be asked — does anybody **doubt** the allegations? It wouldn't be the first, or second, or even third time Trump was caught cheating. Trump's followers tweet "We elected him **president,** not **pastor!**"

Much like shooting a man on Fifth Avenue in broad daylight, he's not going to lose any **supporters** over it.

So what's the big deal?

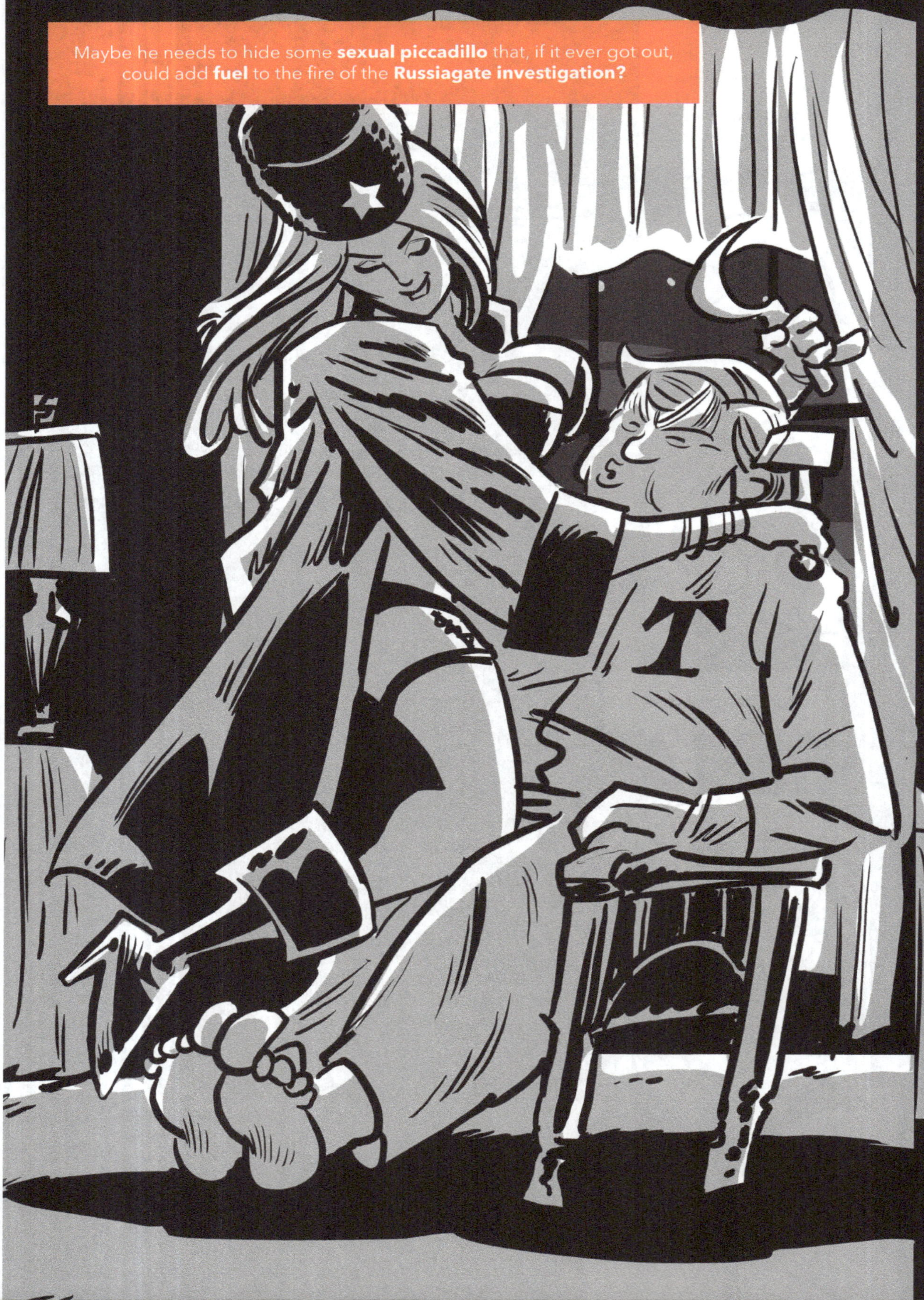
Maybe he needs to hide some **sexual piccadillo** that, if it ever got out, could add **fuel** to the fire of the **Russiagate investigation?**

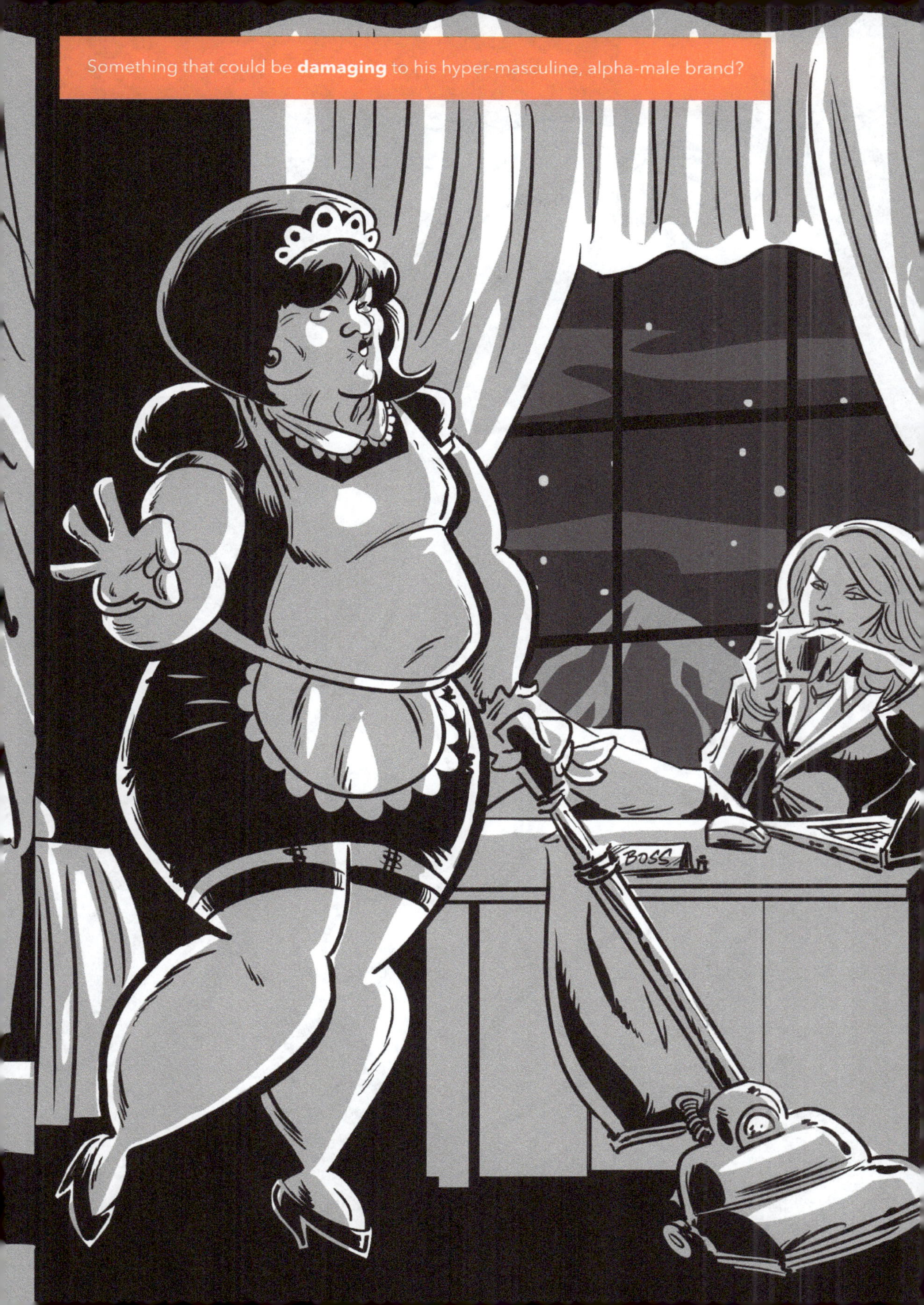
Something that could be **damaging** to his hyper-masculine, alpha-male brand?
BOSS

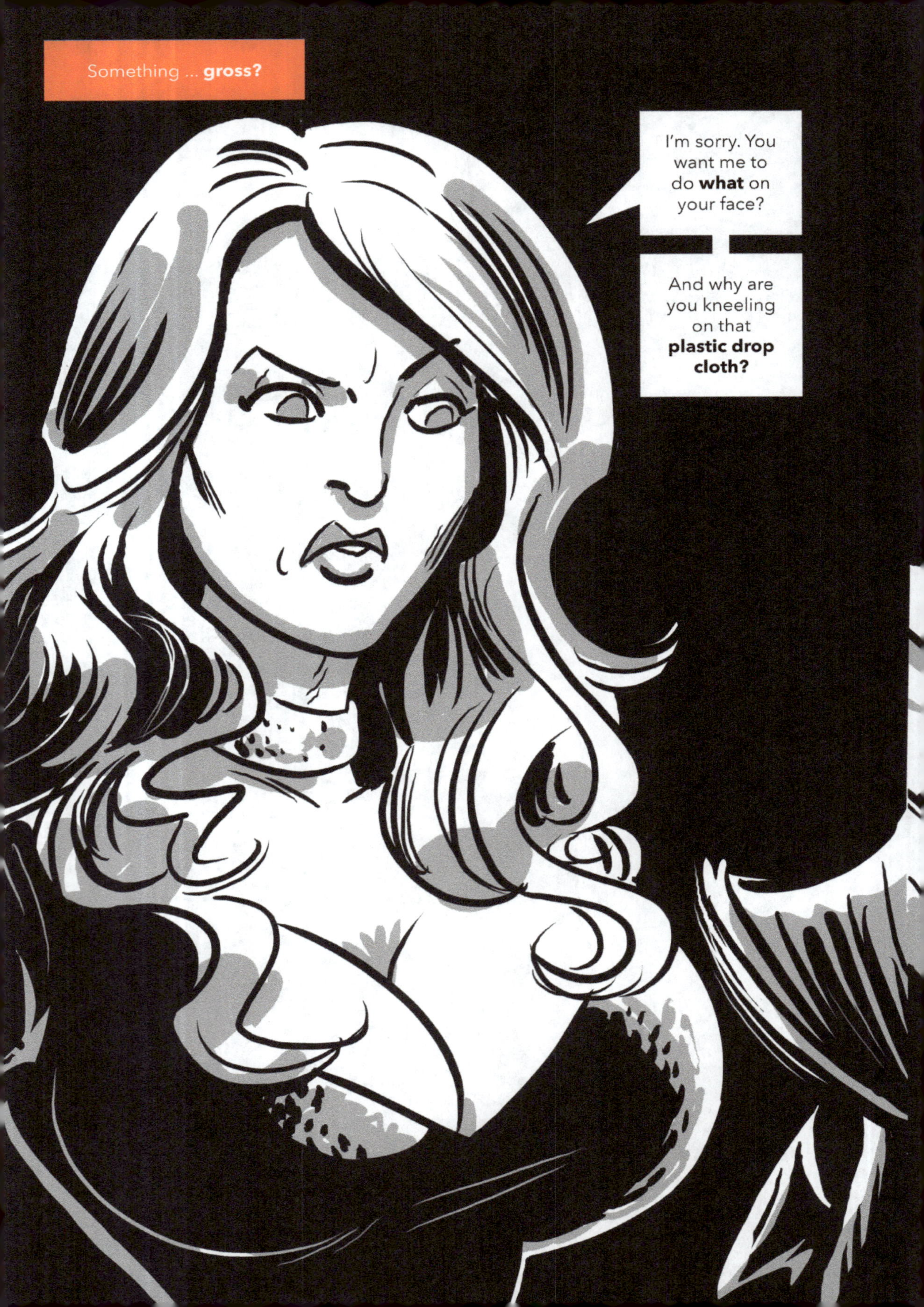
Something ... **gross?**
I'm sorry. You want me to do **what** on your face?
And why are you kneeling on that **plastic drop cloth?**

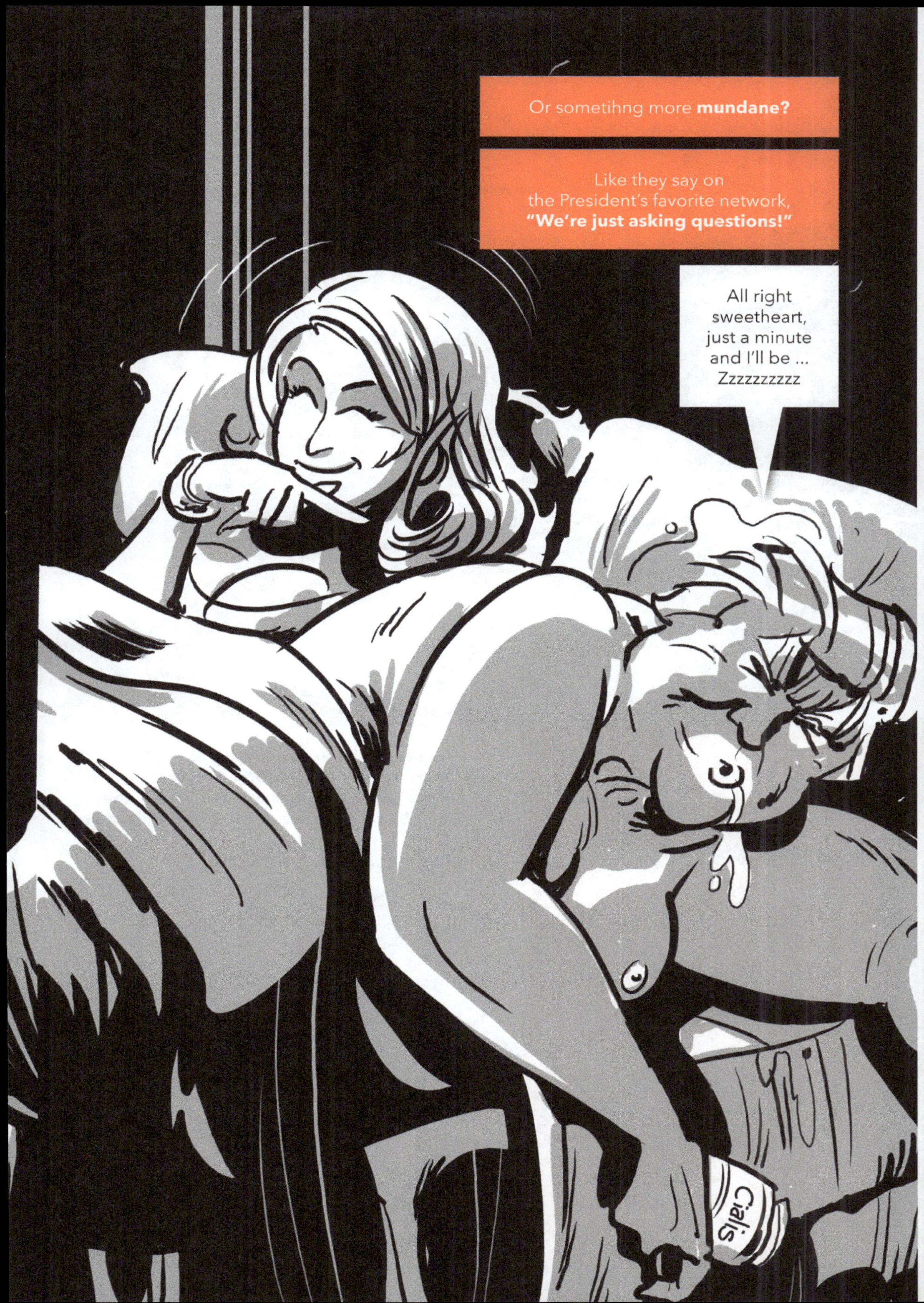
Or sometihng more **mundane?**
Like they say on the President's favorite network, **"We're just asking questions!"**
All right sweetheart, just a minute and I'll be ... Zzzzzzzzzz
Cialis

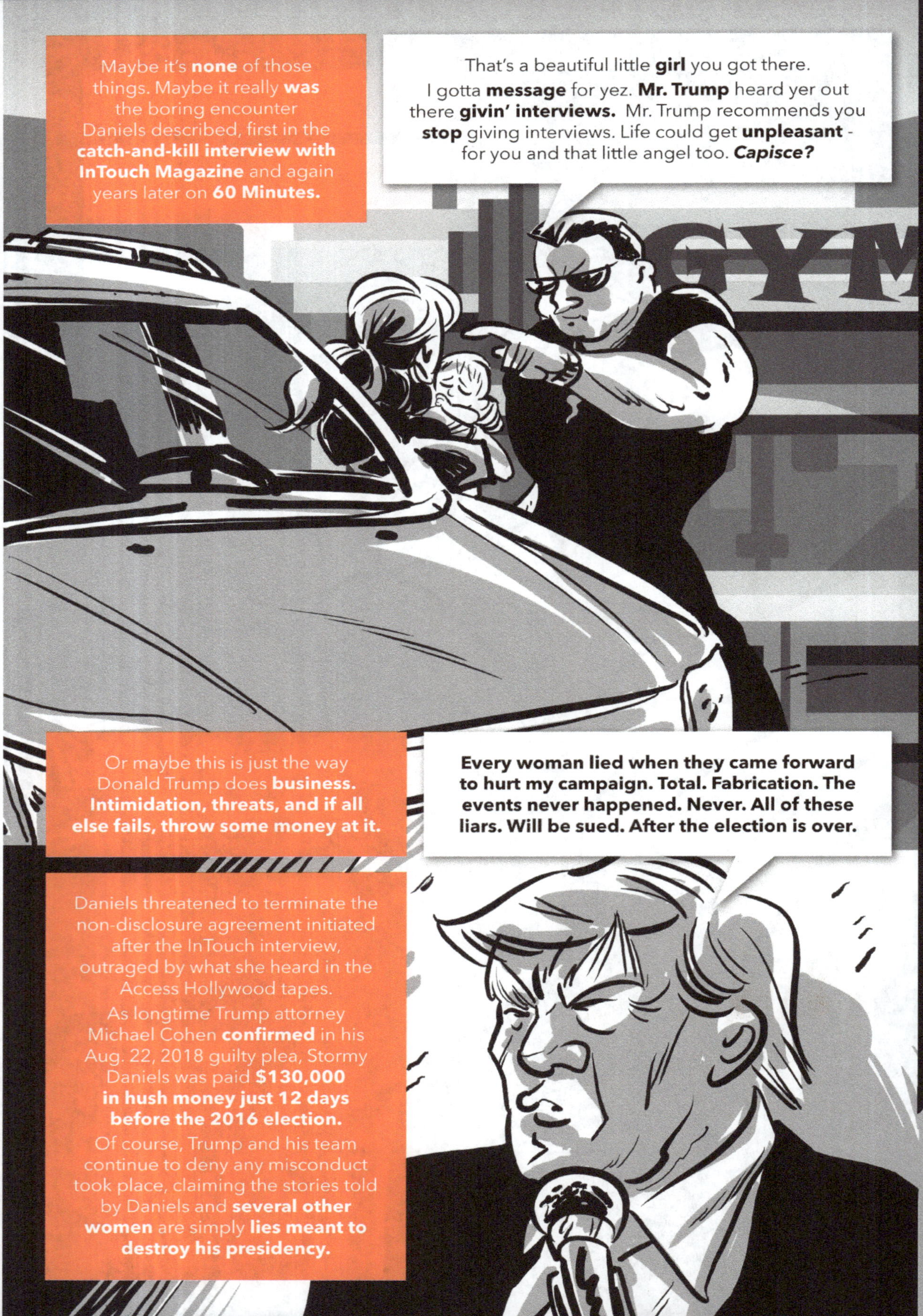
Maybe it's **none** of those things. Maybe it really **was** the boring encounter Daniels described, first in the **catch-and-kill interview with InTouch Magazine** and again years later on **60 Minutes.**
That's a beautiful little **girl** you got there. I gotta **message** for yez. **Mr. Trump** heard yer out there **givin' interviews.** Mr. Trump recommends you **stop** giving interviews. Life could get **unpleasant** - for you and that little angel too. ***Capisce?***
GYM
Or maybe this is just the way Donald Trump does **business. Intimidation, threats, and if all else fails, throw some money at it.**
Every woman lied when they came forward to hurt my campaign. Total. Fabrication. The events never happened. Never. All of these liars. Will be sued. After the election is over.
Daniels threatened to terminate the non-disclosure agreement initiated after the InTouch interview, outraged by what she heard in the Access Hollywood tapes.
As longtime Trump attorney Michael Cohen **confirmed** in his Aug. 22, 2018 guilty plea, Stormy Daniels was paid **$130,000 in hush money just 12 days before the 2016 election.**
Of course, Trump and his team continue to deny any misconduct took place, claiming the stories told by Daniels and **several other women** are simply **lies meant to destroy his presidency.**

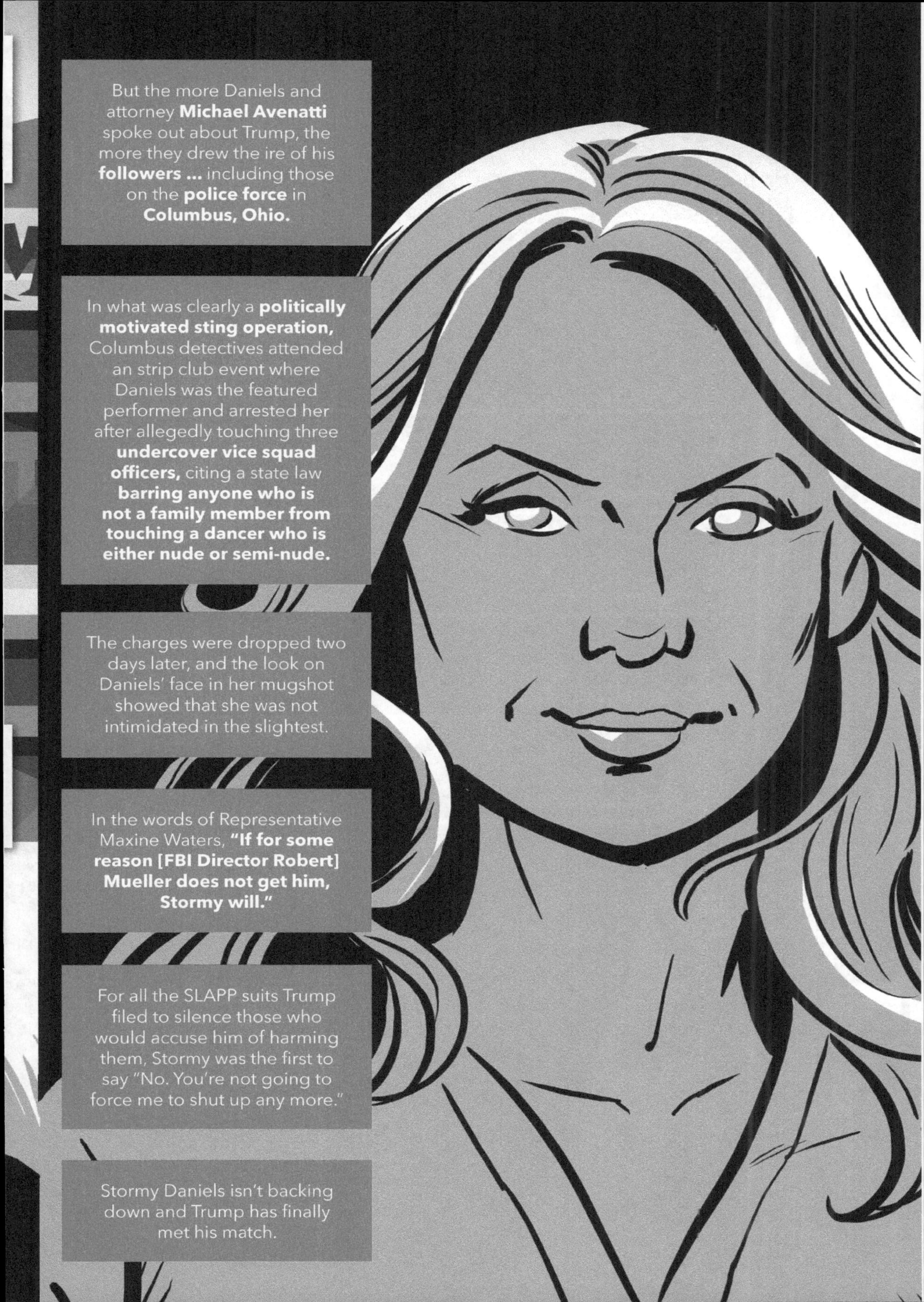
But the more Daniels and attorney **Michael Avenatti** spoke out about Trump, the more they drew the ire of his **followers ...** including those on the **police force** in **Columbus, Ohio.**
In what was clearly a **politically motivated sting operation,** Columbus detectives attended an strip club event where Daniels was the featured performer and arrested her after allegedly touching three **undercover vice squad officers,** citing a state law **barring anyone who is not a family member from touching a dancer who is either nude or semi-nude.**
The charges were dropped two days later, and the look on Daniels' face in her mugshot showed that she was not intimidated in the slightest.
In the words of Representative Maxine Waters, **"If for some reason [FBI Director Robert] Mueller does not get him, Stormy will."**
For all the SLAPP suits Trump filed to silence those who would accuse him of harming them, Stormy was the first to say "No. You're not going to force me to shut up any more."
Stormy Daniels isn't backing down and Trump has finally met his match.

Joe Paradise — Writer

Joe Paradise — Artist

Darren G. Davis — Editor

Michael L. Frizell — Editor

Joey Mason — Cover A

Alternate covers by Joe Paradise

Darren G. Davis
Publisher

Maggie Jessup
Publicity

Susan Ferris
Entertainment Manager

POLITICAL POWER AND CONTENTS ARE COPYRIGHT © AND ™ DARREN G. DAVIS. ALL RIGHTS RESERVED. TIDALWAVE IS COPYRIGHT © AND ™ DARREN G. DAVIS. ALL RIGHTS RESERVED. ANY REPRODUCTION OF THIS MATERIAL IS STRICTLY PROHIBITED IN ANY MEDIA FORM OTHER THAN FOR PROMOTIONAL PURPOSES UNLESS DARREN G. DAVIS OR TIDALWAVE PUBLISHING GIVES WRITTEN CONSENT. PRINTED IN THE USA www.tidalwavecomics.com

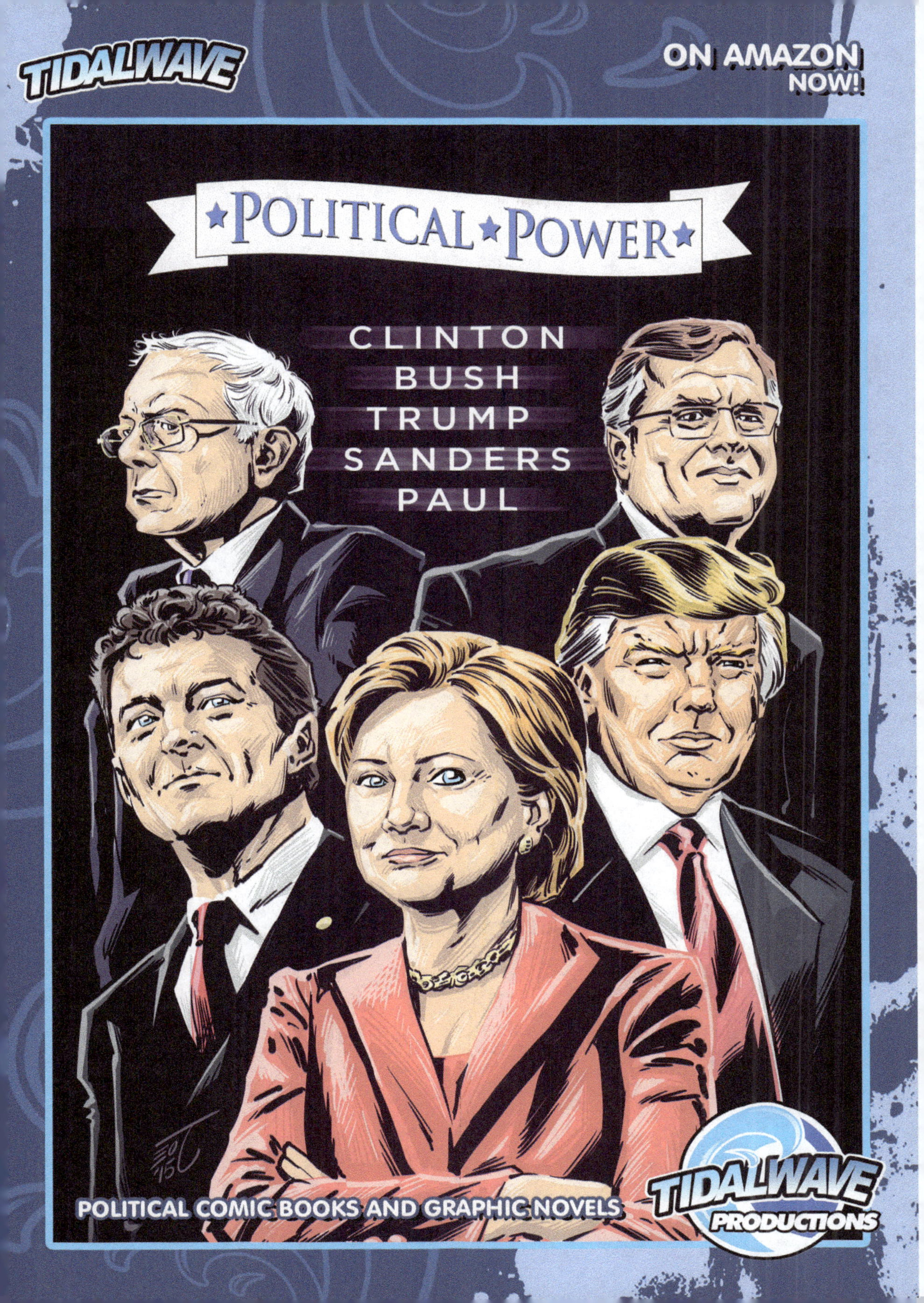
TIDALWAVE
ON AMAZON NOW!
POLITICAL POWER
CLINTON
BUSH
TRUMP
SANDERS
PAUL
POLITICAL COMIC BOOKS AND GRAPHIC NOVELS
TIDALWAVE PRODUCTIONS

INSPIRE
HOPE
CHANGE

The mission of the It Gets Better Project is to communicate to lesbian, gay, bisexual and transgender (LGBT) youth around the world that *it gets better*, and to create and inspire the changes needed to make it better for them.

WWW.**ITGETSBETTER**.ORG

CPSIA information can be obtained
at www.ICGtesting.com
Printed in the USA
LVHW06*2301240918
591276LV00002B/2/P